The "Family Interactive Rating Scale"
A Therapy Tool for Working with Families

A Practice-Oriented Manual for Mental Health Providers

Nate M. Larsen Ph.D.

 www.trafford.com

North America & international
toll-free: 1 888 232 4444 (USA & Canada)
phone: 250 383 6864 ♦ fax: 812 355 4082

Contents

Dedication

****

This practice-oriented manual is dedicated to Lakeland Mental Health Center in Fergus Falls, Minnesota, which has allowed me the freedom to develop and practice this therapy tool with my style of work with children and parents. I also dedicate this to my fellow colleagues, to parents for their input, support, and very positive comments regarding the Family Interactive Rating Scale which I have included in this manual, and to my wife Debi who has once again stood with me, supported me, and assisted me through another venture.

****

Preface

****

The following chapters express my thoughts and experiences while developing and utilizing the Family Interactive Rating Scale (FIRS). Although the central concept is the rating scale, it ultimately encompasses a therapy style that promotes better input from children, fosters increased dialogue within families, and provides a structure with more defined parameters for the therapist when working with families, all in an attempt to help facilitate better change. This is not intended to replace your therapy style with families, but instead suggests a possible supplement to your therapy. As a tool, it can be used as often or as seldom as you, the mental health provider, sees fit. Since developing and using the FIRS I have discovered therapy with children to run smoother and family sessions with children and their parents result in a more productive experience. I hope you find it as helpful and beneficial as I have and that it makes your work with families even more enjoyable.

****

"I think the Family Interactive Rating Scale is very helpful because it helps the children reflect on how they feel they are doing in a nonthreatening way. This also allows both the parents and the child to understand each other's perspectives on how they are doing."

Mother of client

"The Family Interactive Rating Scale is an excellent tool used to discuss and interpret moods, thoughts, and feelings of our children and Nate utilizes this information gathered to measure these. The ratings scale is a superb way to communicate and address topics of concern, along with encouraging open and up front conversations. It has turned out to be an excellent processing tool for our children."

Foster Dad

CHAPTER ONE
Introduction

"I like the fact that with the Family Interactive Rating Scale the kids are actually engaged in the process and they talk and give themselves a score that is more concrete and meaningful to everyone. It's like we're all on the same page and we can understand what each other is trying to say."

Pat Evavold, BA, Mental Health Practitioner and Children's Services Coordinator

****

For years, when meeting with children and parents, I have struggled with how to involve the child in a more understandable and organized manner so therapy does not feel so abstract. As the years passed I found the desire to be more concrete and visible, with more of a "hands on" type of therapy. Maybe it is my age, or maybe it is finding out what seems to work for children works better for me too, but since I started using the Family Interactive Rating Scale (FIRS) I discovered myself appreciating and looking forward more to meeting with children. I believe I have a clearer, more defined direction which the structure of the FIRS provides. Indeed, this structure appears to make sense to all involved and assures our therapy time is more workable and concrete. It is important to keep in mind the FIRS is only one of many tools available for use in counseling with families. It happens to prove effective for me and makes my work with families easier and, I believe, more productive for them. Although no formal research has been conducted with this tool, I have personally utilized it with numerous families in therapy sessions over the past several years. The FIRS does not guarantee change, but I am extremely confident it definitely assists in the process of change. I have discovered sessions seem to go more smoothly, we all stay on track more easily, parents seem pleasantly surprised with the clarity of the child's ratings, and I trust I have more to offer families when they leave. But do not take my word for it, go back to your therapy settings and try it and observe if it works with your style. My goal with this handbook is to keep the explanation brief but still give you a good sense of how the FIRS works. I know today's therapists are busy with many clients and additional paperwork and do not always have time to read lengthy books explaining various processes. Furthermore, I believe the beauty of this method is that it is simple, to the point, easily explained, and implemented quickly within your own settings.

For many years while working with children and their parents, I have used parts of FIRS by asking questions such as, "With ten being the best and one the worst, on a scale of one to ten how was your week?" Or "On a scale of one to ten how is school going, or how are you getting along with your mother, or how did you handle your anger?" Additionally, I have used grades (ABCDF) where I ask children to grade how their week went. Then, I may also have asked parents to grade their child's behaviors. I am sure many of you have done this as well, and that is the essence of the FIRS, but with additional structure. Children are well aware of grading, and I believe to a certain extent, ratings. In fact, they experience it all day in school with teachers, assignments, along with the use of chalk boards and white boards. Therefore, why not take a structured format they are familiar with and bring it into the therapy room. Instead of grading I have found I prefer to use the scale of one through ten. This is due, in part, to the fact it gives me a wider range to rate various functions. Furthermore, it makes sense to kids and is a more universal type grading system for early as well as later grades. In the past several years I have expanded this scaling to include a number of areas, and as you will observe, I have developed a format that provides a consistent way to present scaled questions during the therapy session. Thus, I am convinced, the FIRS provides a structure and framework to guide the therapy process as we discuss problem areas, identify goals, and praise successes. The FIRS can also be tailor designed to each child's unique circumstances, although I still prefer to ask a number of the same questions routinely. The FIRS is based on the belief that a child's input is vital to helping the family make changes. Also, the parent child relationship is not an equal relationship as parents do have more power than their children, and assuming the child is handling this negotiation responsibly, gradually allows for more and more discussion and input from the child as he/she ages. Additionally, the FIRS, in most cases, assumes the parent's perception is more correct than the child's, although there are some exceptions. Ultimately, the FIRS provides a concrete visual framework to guide the therapy process.

Cognitive-behavioral therapy (Friedbreg, 2006; Linares Scott & Feeny, 2006; Pavuluri, Graczyk, Henry, Carbray, Heidenreich & Miklwitz, 2004; Wood, 2006) has more recently recognized the importance of including the family in the child's therapy. In addition, Cognitive-behavior therapy, Solution-focused brief therapy (Iverson, 2002) and Motivational Interviewing (Miller and Rollinds, 2002) have emphasized the importance of using ratings scales and I believe the FIRS blends nicely with these types of therapies. The focus areas of the FIRS tend to be on present functioning, identifying problem areas, talking about what works, and concentrating on changing behaviors and thinking. The rating scale aids us in visually observing improvements in these areas. An example of focusing on changing a behavior would be to ask a child to rate on the FIRS how good they are at "listening and following directions". If they report a six rating, the therapist would then discuss with them what they can do to raise their score higher. Other examples are with cognitions, such as asking them to rate themselves on the FIRS for how well they are doing at "positive self-talk" or with feelings like depression "how happy are you?" or "what number is your self-esteem this week"? The usual emphasis of the FIRS is examining how to change for the positive rather than focusing on the past and where these behaviors and thoughts might have originated from.

Managing anger is another area where many therapists have used scaling. Consider the anger escalation scale, or as referred to by Reilly, Shopshire, Durazzo, and Campbell (2002) the "The Aggression Cycle" where scaling, although with numbers in reverse from the FIRS, is used to help clients become more aware of the level of their anger. Number one indicates very low levels of frustration and as the client escalates, each number represents higher levels of frustration, anger, and eventually rage. This type of scaling and having clients continually refer to their anger as a number, from my experience, appears to assist them in identifying and better understanding their level of anger. For example, when using this scale I will frequently ask the client to indicate where they have been on the anger escalation scale for the week. A client may indicate that they were at a four. We then discuss what occurred that resulted in them moving to a four, how it felt, how they kept it from going higher, what they did about it, as well as how they might have avoided it. Again, scaling provides us a method of discussing and focusing on a rather abstract issue making it more tangible, concrete, and visible.

"A picture is worth a thousand words". How many times have we heard that before? Indeed, observe how much more children are attracted to pictures in books as well as movies and games. If we can portray more abstract concepts into pictures, or even diagrams, we can anticipate concepts being more understandable For example, when I teach psychology courses I often find myself trying to create a picture or diagram to describe something that is abstract, such as when discussing assertiveness, mental health diagnoses, or decision making in relationships. Pictures allow me to more adequately explain these abstract concepts, therefore pictures and diagrams often help us to better understand abstract concepts. In fact the same holds true with the FIRS. If I can persuade a child to understand in a visual concrete way, problem areas, goals, as well as understand successes, and then encourage them to participate in the discussion and write things down, I believe I can better engage them in the therapy process and ultimately be more successful in assisting the child to make necessary changes.

Dr. Phalen (2004) from the DVD "1-2-3 Magic" introduces us to his type of parenting style with comments such as "It almost seems too simple, you may find it almost humorous" but he encourages parents to go home and try it which is how he arrives at the title for his video. Parents come back and say "I can't believe it; it works like "magic". I suspect the idea of counting when children misbehave has been used for centuries, but Dr. Phalen has packaged it in a way that puts substance to it, and I trust I have done this with the FIRS. Indeed, I know therapists have used scaling in many ways with clients for a long time, but my hope is that with the FIRS format there will be more substance and organization to scaling and in a more packaged way make scaling, especially with children, more useful and helpful in the therapy process. The FIRS may seem simple and it is. But, I encourage you as therapists to go back to therapy sessions and the families you are counseling with and try it. I am confident the more you use the FIRS the more second nature it will become and the more smoothly it will fit into your work with families.

An additional step a therapist might take is to send the completed FIRS home with the child. Then, encourage parents to gather with their child before the next therapy session and review how behaviors, feelings, and thoughts are progressing by implementing the FIRS. I strongly believe in the concept of "emotion coaching" (2008, Gottman), i.e., that is parents helping their children to identify and talk more about their emotions, to be a better team member, to read other's emotions more accurately, and to ultimately problem solve and behave more appropriately. This concept is something we as therapists do constantly in the therapy room. To send a simple technique home with children, like the FIRS, for them to review with parents will hopefully result in better communication skills, as well as improved problem solving skills, and handling emotions more responsibly, etc . . . as parents and children work these topics together.

As I have stated in my article published in the Annuls of American Psychotherapy (Larsen, 2010) "this is a simple, hands on, visual, concrete way to work with children and their parents . . . ." The essence of that article was to begin sharing with other mental health providers a method that I have formulated and continue to use in my therapy with families. My hope is that you, as therapists, will discover this method beneficial for you and your clients, and that you can include it with the many other tools you already possess in your therapy tool box. Furthermore, I trust the FIRS can be implemented by mental health practitioners working at skill building as well as school counselors dealing with students. In most cases, I believe the FIRS is most productive when it involves an interactive process within the family, so obtaining both input from the child and feedback from parents is most helpful, although it can be used as a standalone in some cases with some children. Now let us embark on the process of learning how to use the FIRS to assist families in making positive changes.

Points to remember:

1. The FIRS is an interactive tool between child, parents, and therapist.
2. The FIRS is similar to a grading system at school which a child will easily recognize.
3. The FIRS is a concrete, visual, tangible tool to use with families.
4. Similar to the "Anger escalation scale" the FIRS uses numbers one to ten to rate oneself.
5. The FIRS is almost too simple, like the method 1-2-3 magic, but just try it.

"Whiteboard with the FIRS"

CHAPTER TWO

Background

"The Family Interactive Rating Scale is very useful and easy to use with clients of all ages. Children pick up on it quickly and it seems to put them at ease to be given something to do in the therapy session. Parents like it too because it helps them better understand their child's perception of the issues."

Fran Jacobson, MA,
Licensed Psychologist

****

The FIRS was gradually developed over time in response to parents bringing their children into the community mental health center where I have been employed as a psychologist. As stated earlier, I have often used scales and even grades (A =good behavior to F = bad behavior) to aid children and parents to more accurately explain how good or bad things were going for them, or how behaviors were changing. Instead of the usual responses of "sort of", "kind of", "okay", "good", "not so good", the child is encouraged to use the scale/ grade to describe their behavior and feelings. Usually it was done in a rather haphazard manner, a more "off the cuff" way with no particular organization. This un-organized style makes it difficult to compare function-ing from one session to the next. One day I decided to put a scale from one to ten on my white board, which size is about three feet by three feet, in my office. I have used this whiteboard for other psycho education-al purposes in therapy. Next, to help young children un-derstand the concept of the scale more readily, I placed a smiley face ☺ at the top of the ten to signify good behaviors, feelings, and/or thinking and a frown ☹ at the bottom of the white board under the number one as a way of indicating this represented bad behaviors, feelings and/or thinking. Most of the time I explain to children and parents ten means "great" and one means "lousy", as I prefer to use the word "lousy" instead of "bad". (You can use whatever words or phrases you prefer with children.) Later, I decided I wanted to persuade the child to become even more involved, so in addition to obtaining their perspective on the FIRS, I also developed a form on paper. The form replicates what is on the whiteboard and is placed on a clipboard for the child to complete during the therapy session. In addition, on the form I added the words positive next to the smiley face and negative next to the frown face. This makes it more applicable for some teenagers, as well as adults, if I choose to make use of the FIRS with them. Also, on the white board I can easily replace the faces with a positive sign above the ten and a negative sign below the one to make sure they understand the process of rating themselves.

An optional idea to use with the child, which might help the child to better understand and remember the rating scale, would be to divide the rating scale into three parts. The highest and most positive part of the scale would be the green zone, which includes eight, nine, and ten. This part would designate the areas that are going very well and usually the ultimate goal numbers for behaviors and emotions. The yellow zone would be five, six, and seven and would represent cautionary areas or in other words, showing the child they need to be careful. The goal would be to move ratings to the green zone. Finally, the red zone, meaning the danger area, would contain numbers one, two, three, and four, and would specify the area that the child does not want to stay in. So, ultimately in discussions with the child and family, we often discuss how to achieve the green area for all number ratings.

Another method that is optional and might motivate some children is to add up the earned points. This can be totaled each time you meet with the child. As long as you ask the child to rate the same issues at the next visit, the earned points can be compared to the previous earned points. The goal in therapy would be for the child to keep improving their score. Indeed, this could prove helpful as another incentive for the child. I do believe one needs to be careful with this because no one expects children to obtain perfect scores of ten on everything and of course this point system tends to be based on that concept. Improving scores is the real ultimate goal. In other words, a child may have scores eight and above and most of the time this would be considered very proficient, but this then may give a child a score of 135/150. Therefore, I may or may not use the earned points score and I personally may not compare it to the 150, as stated in the above example. Next, I decided to attempt to see the child by themselves before seeing the parent. In doing so I hope to develop a relationship with the child and encourage the child to be more engaged in the therapy process, as well as to gain their personal perspective, thus helping the child to be more central in the therapy process. After completing the FIRS with the child, I would then return to the waiting room and bring their parent/s in to join us by obtaining their feedback and perception of how things are going at home.

The vast majority of the numerous children with whom I have used the FIRS with appear quite honest, as noted by parents who come in to the session later. In fact, most parents seem to agree with their child's comments. From my experience, the FIRS appears to work best for elementary age children, but occasionally it works with teenagers depending on their level of functioning and cooperation. One teenager thought the smiley and frown faces on the FIRS made it seem too immature for him. Therefore, it proved beneficial to place the positive and negative at the top and bottom, rather than the faces. Taking that step seemed to help and elicited more cooperation from him.

I am persuaded using the FIRS as a tool when parents come into the therapy room, makes it easier to conduct therapy, as we have issues and topics already identified by the child on the whiteboard and the clipboard to refer to for discussion. In addition, I am convinced engaging with the child before visiting with the parents allows the child to feel more involved and able to express what they think in the therapy process, and emphasizes the importance of their input. Even when parents disagree with how the child has rated themselves using the FIRS, the outcome results in a less threatening dialogue amongst families, with more emphasis placed on what the child perceives. Sometimes, I will use the phrase "let's see what the boss says" when I escort the parents in from the waiting room. I believe this phrase, or a similar phrase, helps to reaffirm the power structure in the family for the child. Finally, I have also attempted to complete the FIRS with the child and parents together at the same time. Unfortunately, too often the child seems to be uncomfortable giving their personal ratings in front of their parent, and becomes easily worried what parents will think, or the child ends up saying to the parents "you decide". If I notice the parents are beginning to reveal family issues in the therapy session that are no business of the child's, I will then request the child leave the therapy room and I will discuss the issue with the parents. Some of these issues might include such items as marital problems, unusually negative feedback to the child, exceptionally high expectations, and not praising appropriately. On the other hand, if the child is having an especially difficult time accepting feedback from their parents I may ask the parents to step out of the therapy room so I can discuss with the child how they are expressing themselves, pointing out their style of reacting is not building trust with their parents, or the child's reactions are creating more problems. Or, I may emphasize any other issue that I recognize is impeding the therapy process. Eventually, this issue can also be added to the FIRS by asking the child to scale "accepting feedback", then discussing this item with the parents when they return to the therapy room.

After completing the FIRS, first with the child, then with the parent/s, we set goals. This includes discussion about specific ways to increase numbers. I may make a copy of the completed FIRS, send it home with the family including instructions to hang it someplace in the house as a reminder for all, as well as encouraging the family to discuss the progress during the week. (Furthermore, I might also encourage them to complete another FIRS, specifically geared towards identified goals, at home between therapy sessions.) The original completed FIRS is then entered into the child's clinical chart by myself and is easily retrieved for the next session. When the child and parent/s return to continue working in therapy on identified issues/goals, it can be compared with any new FIRS completed. I have confidence using the FIRS as a tool in therapy can facilitate concentrating on a number of childhood disorders including Attention Deficit Hyperactivity Disorder, Oppositional Defiant Disorder, Conduct Disorder, Depression, Anxiety, and Autism Spectrum Disorders. Still, as I have briefly mentioned, I believe the more frequently the FIRS can be used in an interactive process between children and parents (rather than just with children or just with parents), the outcome of therapy will be enhanced, and bring about increased positive change within families.

Points to remember:

1. The FIRS helps to identify issues to talk about with families.
2. Usually, parents seem pleasantly surprised by the honesty of their child.
3. The FIRS helps families relax more as they have something to focus on during therapy.
4. The FIRS gets the child involved by having them copy what is on the board.
5. Using the colors green, yellow, and red, along with adding up numbers, might help the child to better visualize and motivate change.
6. The FIRS may help emphasize family structural issues.
7. The child's copy is readily available in the records for future sessions.

"Therapist and Girl Completing the FIRS"

CHAPTER THREE

Therapy session with the child

"The Family Interactive Rating Scale possesses the ability to make expressing feelings, thoughts, and ideas become visual and concrete, which in turn cultivates higher levels of interaction and discussion and enhances communication. With its universal approach, everyone involved is able to effectively recognize and comprehend the subject of attention."

Andrew Larsen, BA,
Children's Mental Health Practitioner

****

It has been my observation that virtually every time it is the parents who generate the initial appointment for their child, although on a rare occasion it seems to be the child's idea to come for therapy. When I am notified by the front desk that my client has arrived, usually the child is with their parents, although sometimes he/she is with grandparents or foster parents. Typically parents schedule appointments and bring their children in with complaints their child has poor social skills, has trouble in the classroom, has difficulty functioning in some manner in school or at home, or seems too quiet, depressed, and/or anxious.

The first phase of treatment has to do with the diagnostic assessment and, as many of you already know, it is an information gathering session with the goal of establishing a relationship with the family, making a diagnosis, and identifying problem areas to focus on in therapy. The FIRS assists me in gathering more specific information, in a manner I consider to be less threatening, by implementing the rating system, utilizing the white board, using the form completed by the child, and meeting with the child first. Also, from the beginning, the FIRS helps include the child and starts to send the message to the child they are important to the therapy process. With ongoing sessions the FIRS allows the session to be more predictable and consistent for the child as well. Because it is seldom the child's idea to come in for therapy, I also like to put them at ease by meeting with the child first so they can come to understand what happens behind the closed door of the therapy office and thus be less defensive and fearful of the process, as well as see again that their input is vital to making positive changes in the family. The following is a brief step by step explanation of how I use the FIRS when meeting with the child for either the first assessment or in follow up sessions without the parents present.

Step One:

In the waiting room I introduce myself, greet the child and parents, ask to speak with the child first, and usually plan on taking about 20 to 30 minutes. When the child enters my office I spend a few minutes explaining the process of counseling and take steps to establish some type of relationship, thus hopefully begin putting the child at ease. After obtaining basic background information from the child, i.e. who is in the family, where they live and go to school, if they have received counseling before, and what brings them to therapy, I begin the process by explaining how we will proceed with the FIRS.

Step Two:

I hand the child the FIRS form on a clipboard and instruct them to copy whatever I write down on my whiteboard. I inform them that this will provide us with a copy for our next meeting because I will need to erase the whiteboard after they leave, and I will also make them a copy of the FIRS to take home so they can remember what they need to work on. At this point I begin assessing to see if the child is advanced enough in their thinking process to understand the concept of a rating scale and be able to rate their functioning in this manner, especially with young elementary age children. In my experience, I have found that the FIRS can be used most of the time by second grade children and older. (I recently tried to use the FIRS with a 15 year old lower functioning boy, but it was obvious he was unable to comprehend the rating continuum so we stopped the FIRS process, although I did try it again a couple of sessions later when he was not as anxious, and he appeared to have a basic understanding of rating himself.) Also, it is at this point I begin to explain the process of first discussing and talking using the FIRS, and next I will have their parent/s come in to provide their feedback on the completed FIRS. Additionally, I may also, as we talk, not only make sure they are understanding how to complete the FIRS correctly, but also make comments to them such as "it will be interesting to hear what your parents have to say, if they agree or not". Hopefully these comments encourage the child to report more honestly than if they thought their parent/s was not going to see their completed FIRS. On the other hand, it is also possible these comments may inhibit the child from reporting openly about issues. But, my experience has revealed most children are far more likely to be open and honest than not. Throughout this method I want them to begin to understand and experience the importance of their input in the process of implementing positive transformation.

A colleague of mine, Fran Jacobson, a licensed psychologist, has adapted the FIRS slightly by still using the numbers one and ten on the left side of his white board, but then adds a vertical line in between these two numbers so the child is not restricted to all the numbers for scaling, but instead is simply instructed to rate the issue somewhere between one to ten. He has discovered this appears to work better for some kids who might have a bit more trouble with the idea of scaling. Fran has the child place a mark on the vertical line, and then Fran writes in the issue. He does not use the clipboard, but will dictate into his progress notes various ratings so he can have this for the next therapy session. I believe Fran's actions are a good reminder to us therapists that the FIRS can be tailored, not only to what you consider works best for the child, but also what works best for you the therapist. Thanks Fran!

Step Three:

I usually initiate the process with the most non-threatening topics which include school performance and behavior. Although, if I judge these are too threatening, I will start with another topic. I have discovered the activity of completing the FIRS appears to help children open up and become more relaxed about the interview. Furthermore, I recognize the FIRS assists me in obtaining more detailed information from the child. For example, instead of asking the child "How was your week at school?" and they tell me "It was okay", with the rating system I can receive a number such as a six which reveals more. In fact, it allows me to continue discussions to find out why the child rated it a six and not an eight or nine, or is a six higher or lower than what they experienced the week before. Then, as you will notice, it also initiates the opportunity to question what needs to happen in order to raise their rating. Next, I roll my office chair over to my three feet by three feet whiteboard (which is low enough I can continue sitting while completing the FIRS) placing a smiley face at the top left side, numbers ten to one below that, and a frown at the bottom. If it is an older client, like a teenager or an adult, this might be where I will modify the faces on my whiteboard to positive (+) and negative (-) symbols. Next, I continue by explaining that ten is "great" and one is "lousy" and I will be asking them a number of questions on how they believe things are going. I also stress it is important to rate between one and ten which number best represents how they are functioning now. I believe it is also essential to make sure my vocabulary is at the level of the child's vocabulary to guarantee they comprehend me correctly.

Step Four:

With this step I start with the subject of school and say something similar to "How are you handling your school work, or what number best represents your grades these days?" The child will respond and indicate a number and I write the issue "school work" or SW on the whiteboard next to that number. I then make sure they are copying it on the FIRS form that they have on their clipboard. Additionally, I try to use one word or less for each rating to simplify writing, so as not to be too difficult for them to copy, and also to provide more room for writing. Unfortunately, sometimes I forget the abbreviations I have written, but the child will usually remember better than me! The topics and occasional abbreviations listed below are what I typically use in therapy with the child. Again, you may modify this to your child without having to explore all issues and you may also use your own abbreviations. Of course, you can also develop other topics or issues not listed below. It is typical for me to ask the child to rate approximately 15 to 20 issues. The one word topic or issue characteristically refers to how they are getting along with that person, or how they are handling an emotion, or how they are behaving in that setting, etc . . . .

Typical Topics and Abbreviations in Completing the FIRS (no particular order):

School work = SW
School behavior = SB
School kids = SK
Teachers
School lunch = SL
School hallway = SH
Recess
Behavior chart at school = BC
Bus
Mom
Dad
Brother = Bro
Sister = Sis
Siblings = Sibs
Going to bed = GTB
Getting up for school = GUFS
Listening and following directions = LFD
Anger
Worry

Not avoiding = NA
Happy
How I feel = HIF
Accepting feedback = AF
Self-esteem = ES
Living at home = LH
Living at foster home = LAFH
Self-talk = ST
Bottling up = BU
Open
Isolating
Chores
Relaxed
Prayer
Faith
Church
Youth group = YG
Medication = Meds
Friends
Sexual boundaries = SB
Physical boundaries = PB
Trust
Decision making = DM
Respect
Accepting no for an answer = ANFA
Using inside voice = UIV
Feel Safe = FS

Step Five:

As I continue questioning the child seeking ratings for each of the above topics or issues, I frequently ask them if it is getting better or worse. I am confident it is important to emphasize both. For example, if the child says yes, their anger is improving, and they have formerly rated it a three but now it is a six, I would then draw an arrow up from the three to six and write "anger" at six. On the other hand, if the child explains they are having a more difficult time dealing with an issue such as getting into more trouble and behaving with more aggression, and the child indicates their anger has gone from a six to a three, then I put an arrow starting at six to the three with "anger" written at three. I will also use this opportunity to question the child in regard to what they have done specifically to either raise or lower the numbers with this topic of anger. Indeed, I am certain it is very valuable to have the child verbalize clearly why something is working better or not working as well for them. (I also share this with the parents when we go over it.) One important thing to keep in mind is I ordinarily try to portray issues and topics in the positive rather than negative context. In other words, instead of using the word worry I might ask the child to rate the issue of relaxed, with ten being very relaxed and one being not relaxed at all. I simply try to emphasize the positive as much as possible. Finally, I instruct the child to rate themselves overall by giving a score from one to ten. I then circle this number and may put an arrow up or down to indicate where they were before. This way I have one score that illustrates where the child believes he/she is presently functioning.

Step Six:

When I finish interviewing the child, I hope to have a number of topics rated both at home and school, as well as other places such as Grandma's, neighbors, shopping, etc . . . ., and may have some arrows going up and others going down. As I draw the arrows, I am reminding the child our goal is to get the numbers higher in all areas, expressing my hope is they can achieve between an eight and ten. I am also emphasizing that their parents may not agree, but this is what the child thinks, and that is of great significance. On a rare occasion the child rates something, and either claims they do not want their parents to know or I sense some fears of parents knowing how they are rating themselves. I will use my judgment to decide if we should erase the rating, or if I want to consider convincing the child to leave it and discuss it with the parents. For example, if the child rates getting along with mom a three and relationship with dad a nine, and mom is out in the waiting room coming in soon, the child may not be ready to discuss this with mom, which of course tells me something about the home life. Sensing this, I may need to approach this topic more cautiously or discuss it at later time, or mom herself may end up expressing her concern about their relationship.

Step Seven:

The FIRS offers several additional options for use other than simply completing it and obtaining parents' feedback, although I probably engage this the most. One optional method is to calculate the "earned score" and the "total score". As the therapist, you can use one or both. Also, remember that ten is the maximum a child can earn on each rating. Therefore, if you have asked 15 questions then the total score would equal 150. Once the earned score is calculated the therapist can compare this to a score from a previous session, assuming the same questions were asked both the first and subsequent times of administering the FIRS. (Of course, comparing scores needs to take into account the parent's corrections.) The earned score could also be translated to a grade as well, with ten percent representing a grade. For example, a grade of an A would equal any score between 135 and 150, as 15 points is ten percent of 150. Please remember this is entirely optional. You, as the therapist, have a number of choices which include; discussing the ratings, sending the FIRS home with them, adding up only the earned score, adding the earned score and comparing it to the total score, and/or giving them a grade. Using the total score and grade, of course, is always comparing their score to a perfect score which may not be necessary or even reasonable. As a matter of fact, I usually prefer not to get into total scores, but some children may find this more motivating and helpful in their process of making constructive changes. Restating yet once again, you are the one to determine how to proceed, depending on the child.

Step Eight:

At this point, if I observe we have covered all areas, and I have a good sense as to how the child views themselves functioning, I explain I will bring in their parent/s (who are in the waiting room) and with them we can discuss the completed FIRS and discover what they think. At this particular time I may state "Let's see what the boss says about this". If I notice some defensiveness on the part of the child, I will emphasize that this is a good time to practice talking about sensitive issues and start showing mom and/or dad feedback from them can be handled respectfully. Also, I may stress the fact as we get older more and more things should become negotiable, but it is still up to the parents to decide what this may be. Another issue might be with parents. For example, if they are getting "roped into" endless arguments with their child, they may need help learning to say "no more discussion", although this may be discussed with the child outside of the office, then practiced with parent and child in the office. Again, except for some rare instances, I seek to support parents being in charge at home and within the family as much as possible. Furthermore, I never desire to invalidate or take power away from parents by putting them down or belittling them in any way in front of their children.

Finally, keep in mind if this is the first diagnostic session, you may need to meet with the parents alone to gain more information before reviewing the FIRS with them and their child, or at least after the FIRS has been reviewed. You, as the therapist, will need to deem how much you wish to incorporate the FIRS into your sessions. It is also entirely possible the FIRS will be used only after the diagnostic assessment it completed. I personally choose to utilize it as much as possible, as I appreciate the information it provides me and I also trust just implementing the FIRS results in the child being more involved in the process of therapy. Yet again, you may tailor it to what you distinguish as best for each family you counsel.

Points to remember:

1. Use the FIRS with the child to help facilitate understanding where he/she is coming from regarding feelings, thoughts, and behaviors.
2. Use the FIRS with the child first, then together with their parents to discuss issues and struggles the child is experiencing.
3. An option might be to use the FIRS with a vertical line alongside the scale of one through ten, so the child can place their issues next to the vertical line, without the constraints of the numbers two through nine.
4. Use the FIRS as a reminder of what issues need to be worked on by sending a copy of the completed FIRS home.

5. Use the total points of each issue rated on the FIRS as an added motivation for the child to change behaviors, then compare with previous total points from the previous session.
6. Be sure that the child understands that the next step after they rate themselves is to gain feedback from their parents.

"Boy completing the FIRS"

CHAPTER FOUR
Therapy session with the child and their parents

"The Family Interactive Scale is a wonderful tool when working with children and their families. This rating scale is a simple and successful way to help stimulate discussion among family members and their mental health professional. It is definitely an asset in a world where we are under pressure to work more quickly and efficiently"

**Denise Risbrudt BSW,
Mental Health Practitioner**

****

Meeting with children individually is decidedly important. Indeed, it helps assure more involvement as well as developing a sense of ownership, which hopefully provides better results from them. At the same time, engaging with parents is also very significant. Coming into counseling is seldom the child's idea, and oftentimes I cannot rely on just the child's perception, although a surprising number of children do seem to give quite accurate responses to the rating scale when compared to their corresponding parents' later comments. Still, I believe getting parents to react to their child's perception is a crucial part of therapy. It assists in validating the parent as the authority figure and encourages clarifying, both to the child and therapist, which problem areas are of real concern. In addition, it involves the family in the therapy process and dialogue, thus signifying the significance of this particular group of individuals. I rarely meet only with the children or only the parents, although I suppose on infrequent occasions this might be more appropriate.

Indeed, there are special times when how the parent reacts to the child's ratings might seem inappropriate, immature, or abnormal in some way. As indicated earlier, on these occasions I might ask the child to leave so I may, as their therapist, confront the parents on their type of reactions and mannerisms and try to assist them in making positive changes. As I have already noted, I occasionally may not want the child present in order to emphasize better boundaries and help retain parents as valid authority figures. Also, there are sessions when I may ask the parents to leave and speak only with the child as I notice either the parents or the child is becoming overly defensive or unusually angry. Again, I might rehearse and role play with the child demonstrating more appropriate methods, then encourage the child to try these methods as I retrieve their parents and try again to sit together as a family to review the FIRS.

At this point we are prepared to begin the second phase of the treatment session. I have received the child's ratings to the FIRS as well as explored and discussed issues which have increased or decreased in ratings compared to past weeks. Now it is time to have the parents enter into the therapy room and review with them how their child perceives himself/herself functioning and gain the parents' perspective. Once again, if I judge it is necessary to emphasize the authority of parents at this point I may exclaim, "I'll go get the boss and see what she/he thinks of your ratings". Most importantly, I do not want the child to view me as the boss, so family systems can be emphasized as well through this process of utilizing the FIRS.

I should also note here if there are other children with the parents, I may or may not include them in the session to review the FIRS. I use my judgment to determine if I perceive it will be helpful to the family overall. If I sense in any way it will feel overwhelming or overbearing to the child whom parents believe and have identified as needing to change, I would not let the other children be present and I would have them stay in the waiting room. On the other hand, I might allow siblings to come into therapy and then in some form include them in the ratings so it does not appear like we are picking on one child. This is where, as a therapist, you need to stay particularly sensitive to some of the family dynamics and make your decisions accordingly.

Step One:

I proceed by retrieving the parents from the waiting room, where they have been waiting while I have been interacting individually with their child. As we sit down in my office I may start with a little "small talk" then point to the board and indicate that their child and I have been discussing a number of topics and issues. I explain while the child and I talk, I have been writing down the child's ratings on the board, she/he has been copying it on a similar form on the clipboard. I continue by indicating how ten at the top means "doing great" and one at the bottom is "lousy".

Step Two:

I confirm to the parents I will explain each line, but suggest the child correct me if I get it mixed up, or if I forget a particular abbreviation. (I am learning to be more careful of my abbreviations as there have been a few instances when neither the child nor myself can remember what the abbreviations stood for.) I always begin with the top line numbered ten, the really positive stuff, explaining each word or abbreviation that the child has rated as going great. If there are any arrows going up to ten at this time I would explain this means your child believes this issue has improved lately from whatever number the arrow comes from and also discuss why they think is has improved. In other words, what is the child doing differently that results in the child rating the topic higher than before?

Step Three:

As I explain each line and accompanying arrows, I request feedback from the parents to ascertain if they agree with the child's perception or not, and if they agree we continue. If the parents do not accept the perception, we stop and explore what number the parents believe best reflects where the child is at in their functioning of that particular issue or topic. At this juncture the child usually appears to agree with their parent's observation, but if the child does not, this is the time to discuss why or why not they think differently. This is also the point, as it is throughout the entire discussion, to express what needs to occur to receive a higher score. If the child absolutely disagrees with the parent, rather than getting into a power struggle I will suggest to the child that they do not have to agree, but because the parent is the authority, ask the child what they might do to get their parents "off your back" so to speak, in order to achieve a higher rating. This latter occurrence seems to happen more often with a clearly oppositional child or possibly a teenager who is more engaged in their independence.

Step Four:

I proceed by defining and discussing each line with the words and abbreviations that the child and I have discussed previous to the parents entering the room. In addition, I continue to elicit feedback from parents and child to make sure the FIRS fairly and accurately portrays how the child is functioning at this time. If there is an item the parent observes as different then the child, I circle it, sometimes with a different color, with an arrow going up or down to what the parents perceives actually happening. At this point, I also make a "big deal" of any scores the parent scores higher than what the child thought and might ask the parent to tell me specifically what the child is doing that is so appreciated. I also take this opportunity to discuss with the child and parent actions that need to be taken to raise the rating if the parent's ratings are lower than what the child declares it to be. For example, I might state to the child and parent, "What needs to happen in order for a higher rating to occur in this area, such as moving from a five to an eight?" Another example to address might be an issue such as how well the child listens and follows directions. I might ask the child, "What do you need to do to get a higher score from your parents in this area?" Once identified, we might then practice specific steps to begin making those changes. Indeed, I want to continue to elicit responses from the child and keep them engaged in the dialogue, as much as possible. If the parent takes over the discussion too much this could provide another opportunity to have the child leave the therapy room and discuss with the parent how they could respond to their child more appropriately. During this time I am also continually monitoring the child to make sure they are correcting ratings the parents have noted as higher or lower than the child indicated, on their clipboard. This guarantees the child is circling that item and drawing appropriate arrows up or down.

Step Five:

As we continue through the FIRS, we end up with a profile of the child. This profile may be agreed on by parents, or we may finish with a portrait containing a few corrections by the parents, or we may even stop with a portrait reflecting numerous corrections as indicated by parents' responses. Whatever the case, this provides us an opportunity to explore successes and struggles the child might be experiencing and to begin discussing how to rectify different issues that are a problem. We might discover both the child and I have forgotten an issue which the parents have brought up and then can be added with both child and parent indicating a rating for it.

Step Six:

If this is the first meeting with the child and parents, then goals could be developed during this session. On the other hand, if this is a follow up meeting and goals have already been established, then the goals could be rated on the FIRS from both the child's and parents' perspective. Before ending the session I would reemphasize the goals and what areas need added effort. As mentioned previously, it might be useful for the child to receive a copy of the completed FIRS to take home with them as a reminder of our discussion and what elements need to be worked on at home. Remember it is also optional to use scores and grades as you decide how detailed you want to get. A reminder; if you are planning to use scores, make sure to ask the same questions at the next therapy session or comparing scores would be irrelevant.

Step Seven:

We end the session agreeing to return in one or two weeks. For example, I thank everyone for coming, and encourage them to set up a future session at the appointment desk for our next meeting where we will again discuss how things are proceeding using the FIRS. The frequency of the FIRS is optional. It could be used every time or less often depending on the parent-child interaction or how you sense it is being accepted or needed. I truly believe the FIRS is a useful tool to promote structure in the therapy session and I trust it assists in engaging the child in the therapy process more than without its presence.

As I have stated earlier, at times it might be okay to use the FIRS without obtaining feedback from parents. This situation might involve a child with parents requesting the child be allowed to talk with someone else or without parents being involved. Furthermore, the parents may feel the child needs to speak with someone in private in order to deal with a very sensitive issue. It may also be appropriate to utilize the FIRS for teenagers who need to process and work on some issue where parents have agreed to be uninvolved in the process. Finally, I have occasionally employed the FIRS with adults as a way to identify and process how things are progressing for them. I have implemented it with clients who have Schizophrenia or have Borderline Personality Disorder. Again, it is a concrete way to measure success or struggles in various areas. The vast majority of time though, I prefer for it to be a family process where child and parents visit and interact together regarding their issues. I believe the strength of the FIRS is promoting family dialogue, but again you are the therapist, and you conclude how and when to apply it in therapy sessions.

Points to remember:

1. Except for rare occasions, parents are always treated as the authority figures with the last word.
2. As ratings are explained with the parents present, I remind the child to correct me if I explain some-thing incorrectly.
3. If family dynamics make it difficult to continue with the dialogue I will ask either parents or child to step out, deal with the issue, then reunite the family.
4. Parents input that is different from what the child has stated, is recorded on the white board and the form on the clipboard.
5. Goals are set up with the child based on the com-pleted FIRS which includes parents input.
6. Follow up sessions are then scheduled with further use of the FIRS if desired.

"Daughter and Dad Discussing the FIRS"

CHAPTER FIVE

Case examples of children completing the FIRS

"The Family Interactive Rating Scale is a very useful tool for the CTSS program. The rating is helpful for practitioners to know how the parents and client rate themselves. It's an excellent way to communicate and see their perspective. This allows us to know in a short amount of time the areas of concern."

Pep Ross, BA,
Children's Mental Health Practitioner

****

Chapter five includes examples of the FIRS completed by children and adolescents in therapy. For each of the FIRS, I will provide a brief history of the child's family, followed by an explanation of the child's completed FIRS. All five FIRS discussed are found at the end of this chapter in order of their presentation. Information on these FIRS does not represent any particular clients I have worked with, but instead are fictitious and are a compilation of many children and parents I have counseled with over the years, in order to furnish you with a variety of examples.

Case #1 History:

Case number one I will refer to as "Joey" who is in the fourth grade. He lives with his mother and half-brothers and has no contact with his biological father, although his siblings have contact on a regular basis with their biological father. He has been diagnosed with ADHD and is on medication for this disorder. Furthermore, Joey has an Individual Education Plan at school, and has struggled with academics, anger expression, sibling rivalry, attention and focusing problems in school, as well as friendships. His relationship with his mother is not problematic nor does he have relationship problems with his teachers. He appears to be comfortable coming to counseling. Also, Joey is able to articulate his thoughts and feelings quite well, and is visibly proud of the progress he has made so far.

Joey readily adapted to the FIRS. Both times he gave the impression of easily understanding the concept and effortlessly volunteered ratings for the questions I asked him. With Joey, I started with his school performance, as I usually do with most children. Next, I moved into discussing his functioning within his family unit. Finally, we talked briefly about his father. As can be noted on both FIRS and in the explanation that follows, the issue with his father is a tough one for him, especially because his half-siblings have regular contact with their father, but he has none with his. Furthermore, Mom also knows that this is problematic, so one thing we decided was to make a referral to the Children's Therapeutic Support Services program to provide Joey with the opportunity to concentrate on improving social skills, and to afford him an occasion to develop a special relationship with another adult, preferably a male. His mother and I also discussed contacting his medical doctor to make sure Joey is on the optimal amount of medication for his ADHD. It is also possible he struggles with a mood disorder, and this needs to be kept in mind during further contact with him.

Case #1—Joey's Goals:

1. Telling the truth.
2. Manage anger appropriately.
3. Complete school work satisfactorily.

Case #1 FIRS Explanation:

Line 10: Joey has indicated he believes his medication is working very well, his appetite is good, and he is handling his anger very well. Notice the arrow going up from five to ten for anger, meaning it has vastly improved. Additionally, Joey perceives he handles his bus rides fine, his relationship with his mom is great, and he is positive on how he is getting along with step-dad (S-Dad). Notice too, that bus is circled and an arrow goes down from ten to eight, meaning mom believes it does not go quite as well as Joey.

Line 9: He states that his concentration is good, has no problems going to bed (GTB) and his self-esteem is fine. He is also rating himself as happy. Next, notice there are two arrows going up to from line seven, one to concentration and one to happy. Joey believes they have both improved.

Line 8: Joey indicates being able to ignore kids that bug him (including his brothers) on this line, so he is acknowledging some problems, but again minimal.

Line 7: He places school work (SW), sleeping, and getting along with his brother (Bro) on line seven. Notice again that school work used to be at a three; therefore he believes he has improved considerably in his academics.

Line 6: On this line he places getting up for school (GUFS). He is indicating continued difficulty for this issue.

Line 2: Joey places lying on line two. He says he still lies too easily to mom because of worries about getting into trouble and agrees this is an area he definitely needs to concentrate on.

Line 1: He places Dad on line one indicating this is a very difficult and sensitive issue for him to deal with, as he has no contact with his father.

Finally the number six is circled meaning this is the number he believes on average he is at this week, although it used to be a four. (Joey's total score is 144/180.)

****

Case #2 History:

Case number two will be referred to as "Sally" who is in the sixth grade and lives with her mom and dad. Recently she has found out that her father had an affair and her parents were contemplating a divorce, but they are now back together. Dad was initially out of the home but at this time is spending weekends at the house working on bettering his relationship and trust with Sally and her mother. Initially, Sally had a difficult time with this, but her reaction is slowing improving. Before finding out about his affair, her relationship with her father was stable but obviously she has struggled lately. Mom brought Sally into therapy to help her deal with her emotions regarding this upsetting event. In this case, her diagnosis is Adjustment Disorder with Anxiety and Depression. This is Sally's first appointment and counseling resulted in attending only three therapy sessions, as she quickly improved in response to her parents improved marriage.

Case #2—Sally's Goals:

1. Continue to improve mood and lessen anxiety.
2. Improve positive relationship with her Dad.

Case #2 FIRS Explanation:

Line 10: Sally positioned school, riding the bus and getting along with dad on this line. Notice she drew an arrow from line eight to line ten where she placed dad, as she has had some trouble with her relationship with dad (although not significant), but it has improved.

Line 9: On this line Sally placed grades, getting along with mom, and how she is sleeping. All of which are still interpreted as quite good.

Line 8: Sally indicated getting along with school kids (Sk), her brother (Bro), her anger, how happy she is, and her appetite (App) on line eight. She is reporting that these issues are also going quite well and are still in the green zone. Notice again how she has indicated improvement in her mood by drawing an arrow up from line six to line eight.

Line 7: On line seven she indicated her relationship with her sister (Sis), how she feels (HIF), and how relaxed she is at the present time. Once again, observe that she is reporting improvement in her feelings and how relaxed she is. Although there are no very low scores, Sally has indicated she has struggled with her father's affair and her parent's separation, but is now coping better. Her mother relayed no change of perception regarding Sally and seemed to be relieved that her daughter was reporting much improvement in the above mentioned areas.

Again, therapy terminated after only three sessions with Sally, as she began functioning continually better in response to her parents' marriage strengthening and eventually dad moving back home full time. (Sally's total score is 118/140.)

****

Case #3 History:

Case number three will be referred to as "Joni" who is in the seventh grade. Joni was adopted when she was in the first grade and her adoptive parents know little about her biological parents. They do know that her earlier years were fraught with difficulties, including some emotional and physical abuse in a foster home she resided in. Joni is a lower functioning girl, behaving and thinking several years younger than her age. This gets her in trouble both at home and school. She is in special education classes most of the day at school, needs lots of small group and individual help, and is a frustration for her parents who often need to lower their expectations for her. She has difficulty academically and behaviorally, as well as struggling with a variety of social skills. Joni is on several psychotropic medications and her diagnoses include the following; Oppositional Defiant Disorder, Attention Deficit Disorder, and Reactive Attachment disorder. She has been involved with mental health services for many years and recently her mental health therapist has been utilizing the FIRS to help her focus on changing behaviors.

Case #3—Joni's Goals:

1. Increase trust by no episodes of lying.
2. Improve anger management.
3. Improve listening and following directions.
4. No cutting.

Case #3 FIRS Explanation:

Line 10: Joni reported on this line, (meaning everything is going very well) her school work (SW), not stealing (ST), not lying (Lie), getting along with her Dad, and going to bed on time (GTB), as well as ignoring troublesome kids. On the other hand mom reported that Joni's lying was actually at a number six rather than ten.

Line 9: On line nine she indicated good sleep and feeling happy.

Line 8: On this line Joni expressed placement of the bus, trust, mom, and getting up for school (GUFS). Mom's corrections indicated trust still at a number two.

Line 7: Joni designated school kids (SK), lunch behavior, and how effective the medications (meds) were working for her on line seven. She also thought her lunch behavior had improved from a four to a seven, notice mom agreed.

Line 6: On this line she placed how she feels about her family.

Line 5: Joni reported anger, listening, and following directions (LFD) on line five. Notice again mom disagreed, but this time indicated that Joni's anger management had actually improved to an eight.

Line 1: Finally, on line one Joni indicated that her cutting was still at a one, meaning lots of troubles and still resorting to cutting when angry and hurt.

Therapy will be ongoing for Joni, as she needs more time to help her deal with a variety of issues. Mom's input will be imperative as it is still far too early to be able to trust only Joni's reporting. In addition, Joni is involved in the Children's Therapeutic Support Services program to focus on development of identified social skills. (Joni's total score is 148/190.)

****

Case #4 History:

Case number four I will refer to as "Jonny". He is a second grader from a large family, and is a middle child who has been involved with therapy for some time. Jonny recently returned to therapy after about three month's absence, in part to report on the many improvements, but to also begin therapy sessions again. Jonny is on an anti-depressant to assist with mood and irritability. His diagnoses are Disruptive Behavior Disorder and Dysthymia. Sometimes he has primarily behavior problems and other times primarily mood issues with sadness and excessive crying.

Case #4—Jonny's Goals:

1. Continue to improve handling anger.
2. Persist in bettering school behavior.
3. Decrease conflict with siblings.

Case #4 FIRS Explanation:

Line 10: Jonny reported that school work (SW), getting along with students (ST), how he was doing in sports, getting along with Dad, and going to bed on time (GTB) were all going very well on line ten.

Line 9: On this line, Jonny also perceived his behavior in public and getting along with friends as going very well.

Line 8: On line eight, Jonny indicated his relationship with mom, getting up for school (GUFS), and his decision making (DM). Notice he believed he had improved in his decision making from six to eight.

Line 7: He reported school behavior (SB), handling his anger, how happy he was, and the level of trust he thought mom and dad had for him on line seven. Notice again that he also indicated he had improved from four to seven with school behavior, five to seven with his anger, and six to seven for happy.

Line 6: Jonny believed he was a six for how he gets along with his siblings (Sibs).

Jonny's overall score for how he saw himself functioning is a nine, up from what it used to be as a six. Dad agrees with everything except that his anger is being managed slightly better than what Jonny thought, up to an eight. Jonny still has some work to do, but is slowing improving in a variety of areas. Overall, Dad is pleased with his progress. (Jonny's total score is 126/150.)

****

<u>Case #5 History:</u>

"Eric" is a fourth grade boy with a long history of fighting with mom and is case number five. This is his first time in therapy and he comes rather reluctantly. He has recently moved here from another state and his father has not been as close to him nor is he contacting him regularly. Lately he has reported that dad is more difficult to get along with as well, but in the past he has usually believed circumstances were fine with dad. School does not go well for Eric in both academics and behavior, especially with this recent move. Lately he has not had much of an appetite and although he has improved in his mood, he still is not reporting much happiness. Overall he struggles with mood and behavior problems. He has established friendships, although mom does not approve of them, so Eric tends to stay home a lot when not in school. His teacher has called lately with problems on the playground with other kids. His diagnoses at this time are Oppositional Defiant Disorder and Adjustment Disorder with Depressed Mood. He has recently seen a psychiatrist and has been taking his medications which are intended to improve his mood and ongoing sleep problems.

Case #5—Eric's Goals:

1. Find more appropriate friends.
2. Continue to improve sleep, appetite, and mood.
3. Continue developing relationships with mom and dad.
4. Improve academics and behavior at school.

Case #5 FIRS Explanation:

Line 10: Eric reports nothing on this line.

Line 9: He rates school friends (SK), but as can be seen mom disagrees with how things go with these kids, and rates it at four.

Line 8: Eric does not report anything on line eight.

Line 7: On line seven he places his teacher and how his medications (Meds) are working.

Line 6: Eric indicates Dad on line six, but this is down from where his relationship with Dad used to be from ten to a six.

Line 5: Eric's sleep, getting along with his brother (Bro) and his happiness are on line five. As noted his sleep is improving from one to five and his mood is up from one to five.

Line 4: Eric reports nothing on line four.

Line 3: On line three he indicates how school is going and how he is getting along with mom.

Line 2: He reports his appetite on line two, which is obviously not good.

Despite continued problems there have been some improvements. Mom is disagreeing only with how Eric is getting along with other children at school; otherwise she thinks his reporting is quite accurate. She wants him to find new friends that are a more positive influence on him. She is hoping his father begins to regularly contact him again and also believes that the medications are helping in some areas, such as with Eric's sleep and mood. (Eric's total score is 52/100.)

Points to remember:

1. Start at line ten and work your way down with explanations.
2. Keep the child involved by asking for their input, especially when scores are reported higher or lower by parents than the child reported.
3. Find out the parents perspective either as you go down the list or after you are done.

4. Make sure to especially praise successes as you continue.
5. Observe how the parents react to the child's rating of themselves.
6. Set goals based on the child's FIRS profile.

Family Interactive Rating Scale

Name: _Case #1 – Joey_   Date: _____

Earned points _/44_   Total points _/80_

☺ Positive

10 _Med / App / Anger / SK / Bus / Mom / S-Dad_

9 _Concentration / GTB / SE / Happy_

8 _Ignore_

7 _SW / Sleep / Bro_

⑥ _GUFS_

5

4

3

2 _Lie_

1 _Dad_

☹ Negative

Case #1-Joey

Family Interactive Rating Scale

Name: _Case #2 - Sally_   **Date:** _____

Earned points _118_   **Total points** _140_

☺ Positive

10 _School / Bus / Dad_

9 _Grades / Mom / sleep_

8 _SK / Bro / Anger / Happy / App_

7 _Sis / HIF / Relaxed_

6

5

4

3

2

1

☹ Negative

Case #2-Sally

Family Interactive Rating Scale

Name: _Case # 3 -Joni_   Date: _——_

Earned points _148_   Total points _190_

☺ Positive

10 _SW / ST / (Lie) / Dad / GTB / Ignore_

9 _Sleep / Happy_

8 _Bus / (Trust) / Mom / GufS_

7 _Sk / Lunch / Med_

6 _Family_

5 _(Anger / LFD)_

4 _I_

3

2 _↓_

1 _Cutting_

☹ Negative

Case #3-Joni

Family Interactive Rating Scale

Name: _Case #4 - Jonny_   **Date:** _____

Earned points _126_   **Total points** _150_

☺ Positive

10 ___SW / ST / sports / Dad / GTB___

⑨ ___Public / Friends___

8 ___Mom / GWFS / DM___

7 ___SB / (Anger) / Happy / Trust___

6 ___Sibs___

5 _____

4 ___I___

3 _____

2 _____

1 _____

☹ Negative

Case #4-Jonny

Family Interactive Rating Scale

Name: Case #5 - Eric   Date: ———

Earned points 52   Total points 100

☺ Positive

10 ___

9 ⟨ SK ⟩

8 ___

7 | Teacher / Meds

6 | Dad

5 | Sleep / Bro / Happy

4 ___

3 School / Mom

2 Appetite

1 ___

☹ Negative

Case #5-Eric

"Mom and Dad Discussing the FIRS"

CHAPTER SIX

Setting goals and follow up sessions

"This has been a helpful and measurable tool in my Children's Therapeutic Support Services goals meetings that the therapist uses to identify problems and successes and then share it with those present. I've also used this in my weekly CTSS sessions to help me understand the student's perspective on their behavior the previous week and then compare it to the parents or guardians. It's also helpful in reporting data in my progress notes. Very effective!"

Marty Soenksoen, BS,
Children's Mental Health Practitioner

****

As indicated earlier, the FIRS can be implemented during the initial assessment to help clarify and set goals, and/or in follow up sessions once goals have been set to discuss ongoing changes in functioning. Depending on how the sessions transpire, I may establish goals the first session with the family or I might develop them in the second session, which ever the case, I do believe clearly defined goals help clarify and create a more concrete direction for therapy. More and more as therapists we are required to have goals that are measureable and time limited. The FIRS is certainly not the answer to writing specific goals, but I do trust it can be beneficial in the process.

Step One:

After completing the FIRS with the child and parents, it usually becomes apparent what areas of functioning need to be addressed. Quite often target areas include lowest scores that need to be focused on. Indeed, often times these are scores in the range of five to six or less, also referred to as the yellow or red zone, depending on the issue. At this time I will begin to focus in on several areas that need to change and do my best to encourage the child to agree with these goal areas. Furthermore, I may discuss the goal from a basic stand point such as "No out of control anger episodes for a period of two weeks" or I may state the goal as "Achieve eight instead of a four on the FIRS regarding anger control, as reported by parents in therapy, for a period of two weeks". Once the goals have been identified, (and I usually like to identify at least two or three goals) I take out the "individual treatment plan" signature sheet and request the child and parent sign. Signing this means we have discussed and agree with the goals identified. Additionally, I check with the child to make sure they know what they are signing, and if they are not clear, I will say to the child, "This is an agreement. It means by signing your name you are promising to work on these goals." Thus, I try to emphasize the seriousness of the process and obtain commitment.

Step Two:

In regard to follow up sessions, I might obtain a copy of the FIRS from the previous session before I meet with the child. In our agency all client notes are kept in electronic medical records, but paper copies can be made. For best results this should be done before the child enters the therapy room and this copy should not be seen by the child until after they have completed their next FIRS. If I decide to compare scores, I need to make sure I ask the same questions about the same issues. Likewise, one could either compare specific issues or earned scores. For example, maybe the child earned a score of 120 on the previous FIRS, which can be compared to a higher score, (hopefully) as it is completed during the next session.

Step Three:

I have never indicated to families ahead of time the number of follow up sessions we are to pursue. Instead, I will usually explain to the family I will evaluate each session one at a time, explain my suggestions, etc . . ., and this could turn into a few or many sessions, but ultimately the parents are in charge of how many sessions we attend together. Again, this emphasizes to the child that the parents are the persons who decide in the family. Each session is usually 45 to 50 minutes and is scheduled every other week. If parents and I perceive the need, or problems are particularly out of control, weekly sessions may be scheduled. Also, at this time I may also suggest other mental health services for the child, such as a referral for a medication evaluation. Or, I might propose Children's Therapeutic Support Services to work on social skills, children's mental health case management, etc. Unless there are problems at the front desk with scheduling, I try to allow the family to handle rescheduling themselves. I am continually trying to empower the child and parents throughout the therapy process.

I have utilized the FIRS numerous times over a number of months with the same child, and other times I have used it less often. Again, it depends on what you as the therapist decide will benefit the child and parents the most, and how easily the child is able to express themselves. I cannot emphasize enough that whether you use the FIRS in therapy, how often you use it, what issues and topics you choose to have the child rate, and what you do with it after it is completed are all dependant on you as you tailor it to the family you are working with. Indeed, the FIRS is another tool to bolster your therapy toolbox.

Step Four:

Another way I like to apply the FIRS is with the Children's Therapeutic Support Services program. If I have made that referral and the child has been paired with a mental health practitioner to work on specific social skills development with the child out in the community, then goals need to be established and reviewed every three months or sooner with myself, the practitioner, and the family. When the family comes in for their appointment, I once again prefer to meet with the child first along with their CTSS practitioner and possibly their mental health case manger. After we have completed the FIRS, including rating their goals, the parents are brought into the session to review the FIRS with us to see if there have been any improvements. If necessary, goals are continued and/or changed with the idea that the child will continue to work on social skill development. It is presumed the child will return in a few months to review goals again. Sometimes I may continue to work with the child and parents in therapy as well, and may use the FIRS as I meet with them.

Points to remember:

1. Clear, specific goals are helpful, and obtaining the child's commitment to working on them is paramount.
2. Remember, this is a joint venture with child and parents, even though you might meet separately with the child first.
3. As indicated, the FIRS is to act as a catalyst for dialogue between child and parents.

4. Again, observe the family dynamics when going through the FIRS together in order to help facilitate change if necessary.
5. Be sure to handle the family session in a manner that is encouraging and focuses on the positive, at the same time identifying areas that need work.

"Couple Completing the CIRS"

CHAPTER SEVEN

Also Included

Couples Interactive Rating Scale

"I really enjoy using this tool and find it enlightens couples in therapy and also enlightens me in my role as their therapist. Having each partner complete this apart from the each other then share them in session together I believe is both stimulating and helpful in the healing process."

Nate Larsen, Ph.D.,
Licensed Psychologist

****

Throughout my history as a therapist I have worked with couples in relationship/marriage counseling, as well as with individuals in group therapy. I have utilized many concepts from the Cognitive-behavioral approach including theoretical ideas from Solution-Focused therapy. Because I counsel with many more children and their parents, I found myself initially developing the FIRS to assist in the therapy session. As time passed I found the need to use some type of rating scale with couples and groups as well. To date, although I have not used it as extensively as the FIRS, another "tool" I have developed is the "Couples Interactive Rating Scale" or CIRS. The CIRS facilitates my efforts with couples as well as group therapy. In fact, it is used to promote discussion and dialogue regarding successes and struggles in relationships and with other issues. Furthermore, it can also be implemented to not only compare scores between members, but also compare perceptions regarding improvements or declines in areas of the relationship over time. Again, as with the FIRS, I believe the CIRS helps make the counseling session more concrete and less abstract and yet still allows for the process of talking about feelings, hurts, success, and desires for change. It is based on the concept of "perception is reality" so each person's perception is important and vital to helping them make changes.

Step One:

A therapist could utilize the CIRS to help couples compare how they report things before problems developed in their relationships and how they perceive these issues to be at this point in time. As a therapist, I have usually applied the CIRS after I have met with the couple several times and developed an understanding as to areas of concern that the couple has labeled and are working on in their relationship. For example, let us say during therapy we have discussed and worked on an area the couple has identified as "conflict management". We might begin with psycho education regarding anger management, the importance of not trying to solve problems when becoming more and more angry, taking time-outs, and the importance of returning and talking again to resolve the issue once emotions have cooled. After they have worked on this in therapy and at home for several weeks or more, I can use the CIRS to discover with the couple how they believe things are improving in the area of "conflict management" by having them rate themselves in this area.

Step Two:

Again, the CIRS can be used to identify how, on a scale of one to ten with ten being great and one being lousy, things are improving. This then allows me to discuss with the couple what steps they want to implement in order to improve the issue or understand why it has not improved. I hand out the CIRS to each partner and ask them to write on the line labeled A on the CIRS form, the word "Conflict", and as can be noted, there is room for a total of five issues to be measured and discussed. I request the couple not sit next to each other during this exercise so they cannot see how each other are completing the form. Additionally, I ask them to rate on a scale of one to ten how the issue of conflict is being managed in the relationship since we last met together. I also request they rate how it appeared several weeks or months ago when we last met. In the case of the CIRS, I do not utilize the whiteboard, using only the two clipboards with the forms for each partner to complete. The following are examples of some issues that might be rated by couples on the CIRS.

Conflict management
Parenting
Communication
Control
Safety
Trust
Depression
Intimacy
Household chores
Anger
Anxiety
Friends
In-laws
Hobbies
Faith
Money management
Or whatever issue you find unique to your couple in therapy

Step Three:

During the counseling session I direct the couple to indicate an N for "Now" and a B for "Before" below each letter and issue. For example, one partner might be putting a B at four and an N at seven, while the other partner may place B at three and an N at nine. Next, I ask them to share and we discuss why conditions have improved, what they are doing differently, and how they might keep this positive process improving. If the situation is not progressing for the better, we discuss this, what has caused this, and how they could fix it. Then, another question to ask might be why one partner rated it now at seven and the other partner rates it nine. It might be after discussing it they actually share the same view and seven and nine essentially mean the same thing. On the other hand, it might be for different reasons too, and that could then become part of the dialogue and an issue to continue focusing on to help them make positive changes. The real key is to help them identify their perspective then dialogue about it.

Step Four:

The discussion continues with other issues identified as B and N and again viewing how things have changed, if they have changed, and how to keep things moving in a positive direction. The rating scale makes it easy to understand the concept of "what needs to happen to achieve an eight when now it is a four?" If scores have become more negative, then this too needs to be addressed, and processed with the couple in regard to what has transpired to make this situation arise and how they can keep this from occurring again. Borrowing the concept from Solution Focused Therapy (Iverson, 2002), the focus is mainly on what has worked and what the couple could apply in order to guarantee it occurs more often.

Step Five:

An option, if the therapist desires, is to add up the Bs and Ns and two scores can be achieved out of a total score which would be the sum of ten times however many issues you have asked them to rate. The scores can be discussed as the couple continues to make attempts to move in a positive direction with their relationship. Also, as with the FIRS, a copy of the CIRS can be made for the couple to take home with them to have a visual reminder of what issues need to be worked on and to practice skills identified in therapy in order to raise scores higher by the next time we meet for a therapy session. In addition, the CIRS can be implemented as often or as seldom as the therapist desires, depending on the therapy session and how easily couples are able to discuss their issues that demand changing.

Step Six:

The CIRS can also be used in group therapy. I have utilized it in the Domestic Violence therapy group I facilitate each week. I have handed it out to group members then asked them to write in the issues at the top of the form they might be dealing with in their relationships such as; Controlling, Managing Anger, Trust, and Safety. Other topics can be focused on as well. I like using this form after the group members have had a chance to work on these issues so that they can compare "before" (B) and "now" (N). Once they have completed the CIRS we then go around the room and each person reports how they believe they have improved or not improved over the last weeks. It provides me and other group members a chance to ask what has worked to improve scores and what has not worked. Overall it indicates a concrete picture of change and a chance to dialogue regarding making positive changes.

As a side note, the CIRS could be used in individual therapy as well when measuring before and now, especially regarding relationship issues focused on in therapy.

Points to remember:

1. Much like the FIRS, the CIRS provides a visual concrete way of discussing abstract concepts.
2. The CIRS helps to promote dialogue between couples to help promote change.
3. The CIRS can be used either at the beginning of or in the middle of therapy to discuss change.
4. As with the FIRS, the focus in therapy should be on the positive as much as possible, such as, what has worked in the past or what would work in the future to raise scores?
5. Use the CIRS with group members or in individual therapy to help measure change and then dialogue about these issues regarding what has worked to promote improvement.

"Men's Group Completing CIRS"

"Case examples of couples and group member completing the CIRS"

"These examples are included to help give you an idea of how to implement the CIRS. Again as with the FIRS, there is lots of room for creativity"

Nate Larsen Ph.D.,
Licensed Psychologist

****

In chapter eight I have included CIRS completed by two couples seeking marriage counseling and a group member from a domestic violence program. As you will note, both partners complete the CIRS and only one group member completes it. In addition, I will give a brief history of each couple, and the group member, and an explanation for how they have completed the CIRS. At the end of this chapter the completed CIRS, in order of presentation, will be displayed. Again, as with the FIRS, these examples are fictitious and are a compilation of couples and group members I have counseled with in therapy over the years and in no way represents a particular couple or person.

Case #1 History:

The couple for case number one will be referred to as "Julie" and "Richard". They have been married approximately ten years, have two children, and both work at full time jobs. In the past several months partner Richard has found out that Julie has been having an affair with a man from their community. Richard found out about it through checking her cell phone history and although Julie initially denied it, she eventually admitted to the affair and subsequently has terminated the relationship with this other man. Richard has been devastated by this and they are now separated. They have decided on counseling because, as time passed, Richard claims he still loves Julie and wants to see if the relationship can be restored. At this time Julie is staying with her friend, trying not to pressure Richard. She is also attempting to see their children when she can, and is more than willing to participate in therapy to see if she can regain Richard's trust for herself and ultimately be able to move home again. They are spending limited time together, mostly centering on the children and household issues. I held sessions with them several times, and then decided to have them complete the CIRS to better understand their perception of how they perceive themselves functioning in their marriage, and to find out if any progress is being made as they work towards spending more time together.

Case #1 CIRS Explanation:

During the therapy session I handed Julie and Richard a clipboard with a blank copy of the CIRS clipped to it. I then asked them to be seated apart from each other so neither could see how the other was completing the CIRS. When they were ready, I requested they write five topics above each of the letters A, B, C, D, and E on the CIRS. I chose these topics based on the conversations we have had in our previous therapy sessions. The five topics were Communication, Trust, Parenting, Problem Solving, and Togetherness.

Richard rates their communication before therapy a three and now at a seven. He rates the trust in the marriage before at a nine now at a five. Regarding parenting, meaning parenting together as a team, he rates at a four before and now at an eight. Problem solving between the two he sees before at a two and now at a seven. Finally, Richard perceives their togetherness in the marriage before at a one and now at a six. Overall you can see there is some improvement in certain areas but a decline in other areas.

Julie rates their communication before at a three and now at an eight. She describes their trust before at ten and now at a three, where as parenting together as a team she rates before as a four and now a six. Julie decides to rate problem solving before at a three and now a six. Finally, she perceives togetherness in their marriage going from a three to a ten. Notice they both observe significant improvement in their communication, a notable decline in trust, improvement in parenting, some growth in problem solving, and finally significant betterment in their sense of togetherness. Also notice their N scores are identical at 33 but their B scores are slightly different. Adding up these scores is optional; it is just another way to discuss changes, differences, and perceptions in the marriage. This exercise promoted good discussion and seemed to bring about a better awareness of where each of them felt they were in the relationship. In a visual way it has shown them areas of successes and areas that still need continued focus.

****

Case #2 History:

In case number two the couple will be referred to as "John" and "Mary". They have been married four years and this is John's second marriage. He has his child with him from his first marriage, and now Mary and John have been trying to become pregnant, but have been unable to conceive which has created increased tension between them. They experince a lack of communcation, as well as John's in-laws are creating problems by interfering too much. Mary is ultimately feeling less and less connected to John, resulting in thoughts and talk of divorce on her part.

Case #2 CIRS Explanation:

Again, during the therapy session I handed John and Mary a clipboard with a blank copy of the CIRS clipped to it. Next I requested they be seated apart from each other so neither could see how the other was completing the CIRS. When they were ready, I asked them to write five topics above each of the letters A, B, C, D, and E on the CIRS. As in case number one, I chose these topics based on the conversations we have had in our previous therapy sessions. The five topics were Space, In-laws, Negotiating, Marriage, and Pregnancy.

Mary rates how her space is respected by John as an eight whereas before it was a five. John says the space issue has increased to a nine from a four, so John is reporting slightly more improvement than Mary, but both are indicating significant growth. Regarding John's in-laws and how the situation is being managed, Mary reports it is at a seven whereas before it was a three. John also claims it is now at a seven after rating it previously as a four. Concerning the couples ability to negotiate, Mary indicates it has become better, moving from a three to an eight and John also senses it has grown from a three to an eight, so both are seeing it as greatly improved. With the overall quality of their marriage, Mary feels it has improved from a three to an eight and John is reporting similar growth from a four to an eight. Finally, as far as both of them dealing with the pregnancy issue, Mary indicates it has improved slightly from a four to a six, whereas John feels it has improved from a two to an eight, significantly more than Mary. One can also note that their total N scores were similar with Mary at 37 and John at 40. Their total B scores were even more similar with Mary reporting an 18 and John a 17.

Overall both Mary and John see significant positive growth in a number of issues they have been working on. Both agreed to continue in therapy and keep focusing on these areas. The CIRS allowed us to review what was helping them improve and how that was different from therapy before. I strongly encouraged this couple to continue the direction they were heading, giving them lots of praise for the progress they had made thus far.

****

Case #3 History:

Case history number three involves a man, a group member from the Domestic Violence Group Therapy program, and he will be referred to as "Mike". Mike was separated from his girl friend for six months after a domestic assault which resulted in a restraining order being placed on him. After the restraining order was dropped he moved back in with her and is reporting that so far the relationship seems to be going well. He has worked hard in group on not being controlling, managing his anger, and dealing with issues overall in a more assertive manner. At this point he is about half way through this treatment program.

Case #3 CIRS Explanation:

In the case of using the CIRS in group therapy, I handle it much the same. I pass out the CIRS form and ask each person to fill in the top five issues. The particular items I selected were issues we had been working on in group for the past several weeks. The five topics included Control, Trust, Safety, Respectful, and Managing Anger. In this type of setting it does not matter as much if group members notice how other group members complete the CIRS form because the information does not apply to them, as it applies more to their individual relationships outside of group in each of their individual settings with other people. Still, gaining feedback from each other in group is part of the therapeutic process so group members reacting to each other's rating is encouraged as long as it is done respectfully. I also prefer to have all group members respond to one issue at a time rather than each member reporting all their scores at once.

Mike reported the following scores after completing his CIRS. He also gained feedback from me and other group members with each issue presented. In regard to control he rated himself an eight now and a three before. With trust Mike reported that it had really fallen from ten to a three, safety improved from a four to a six, and being respectful from a three to an eight. Finally, managing his anger moved from a three to a seven. It would have been interesting to also have his girlfriend complete this form, but she was not available, so in group we relied on feedback from the others as well as me. Mike clearly has a lot of work to do in the trust category, but hopefully with time he will be able to build on this and slowly keep improving that number as well.

Points to remember:

1. Ideally the CIRS is used in a setting with couples so both partners can give and receive feedback on how issues in the relationship are progressing, but it can be used in group therapy settings as well.
2. The CIRS allows the therapist to tailor this tool to the issues the couple is focusing on in therapy.
3. The ten point scale allows for visual clarity regarding the improvement within the relationship.
4. The CIRS is a quick tool to include in therapy as often as desired.

Couple's Interactive Rating Scale

Name _Case #1 - Julie_   Date _____

N points _33_   B points _23_   Total points _50_

	A Comm.	B Trust	C Parenting	D Prob. Solv.	E Together
Positive					
10		B			N
9					
8	N				
7					
6			N	N	
5					
4			B		
3	B	N		B	B
2					
1					
Negative					

Case #1-Julie

Couple's Interactive Rating Scale

Name _Case #1 - Richard_ Date _——_

N points _33_   B points _19_   Total points _50_

	A Comm.	B Trust	C Parenting	D Prob. Solv.	E Together
Positive					
10					
9		B			
8			N		
7	N			N	
6					N
5		N			
4			B		
3	B				
2				B	
1					B
Negative					

Case #1-Richard

Couple's Interactive Rating Scale

Name _Case #2 - John_ Date ———

N points _40_ B points _17_ Total points _50_

	A Space	B In-laws	C Negotiate	D Marriage	E Pregnancy
Positive					
10					
9	N				
8			N	N	N
7		N			
6					
5					
4	B	B		B	
3			B		B
2					
1					
Negative					

Case #2-John

Couple's Interactive Rating Scale

Name _Case #2 – Mary_ Date _____

N points _37_ B points _18_ Total points _50_

	A Space	B In-laws	C Negotiate	D Marriage	E Pregnancy
Positive					
10					
9					
8	N		N	N	
7		N			
6					N
5	B				
4					B
3		B	B	B	
2					
1					
Negative					

Case #2-Mary

Couple's Interactive Rating Scale

Name __Case # 3 - Mike__ Date _____

N points_____ B points _____ Total points_____

	A. Control	B. Trust	C. Safety	D. Respect	E. Manage-Anger
Positive					
10		B			
9					
8	N			N	
7					N
6			N		
5					
4			B		
3	B	N		B	B
2					
1					
Negative					

Case #3-Mike

CHAPTER NINE
Wrap-up

"I have found the Family Interactive Rating Scale especially effective in providing my adolescent clients with a concrete manner in which to discuss their thoughts and feelings, as well as identify improvement in how they feel, think, and cope with various life stressors. Additionally, the Family Interactive Rating Scale has offered a solid structure for sessions that my clients can come to expect, which appears to reduce their anxiety and foster more open discussion."

Jake Walsh, MSW,
LICSW, Therapist

****

Well, there you have it; the FIRS and the CIRS to bolster your therapy toolbox. The FIRS is geared towards working with parents and children and the CIRS with couples. Indeed, I believe the FIRS is especially important when counseling with younger children who are more concrete in their understanding, but both tools' universality allows them to be utilized with teens, and some adults as well. The FIRS provides extra structure and parameters for assisting children in talking to and identifying problem and success areas. Parents are often heard in therapy, but unfortunately their children are not heard as often. This tool addresses this issue by providing a viable method of obtaining a child's input. It can be utilized as often as you like with the children and parents that you see and the FIRS can also be compared to previous ones completed with the child, so everyone can work towards more and more positive changes providing consistency and continuity while working towards goals. What is especially useful with this tool is it generates dialogue between children and parents. Also, as noted, the CIRS helps facilitate dialogue regarding issues in relationships as well and makes it easy to discuss levels of improvement in the therapy session.

But, do not take my word for it, go back to your clients and give it a try. First meet with the child and complete the FIRS by having them rate a variety of issues. Then gather with the child and parents and review it with the family as you identify problem areas and set goals to work at changing how children and parents operate. Utilize the FIRS several times with a family so you can aid them in seeing concrete visible ways behaviors can positively change and families can learn to experience happier relationships with each other. And do not forget to try the CIRS if you happen to be working with couples or in groups. It is a nice addition to your therapy sessions and assists in the review process. Remember, earned and total scores for both tools are optional; you determine how far to take this. I trust you will discover it is a valuable tool to generate dialogue between partners and within families. Feel free to copy the FIRS and/or the CIRS at the end of this manual or create your own.

Points to remember:

1. You can use it once at the beginning, occasionally as you deem necessary, or each time you see the child to measure success.
2. The FIRS and CIRS are designed to be a family affair.
3. Include these tools in your therapy tool box and start utilizing them today.

References

****

Friedberg, R.D. (2006). A Cognitive-Behavioral Approach to Family Therapy. *Journal of Contemporary Psychotherapy*, 36,159.

Gottman, J.M. (2008). *Research on Parenting.* Retrieved June 25, 2011, from www.gottman.com/parenting/research

Larsen, N. (2010). Using the "Family Interactive Rating Scale" in Family Cognitive—Behavioral Therapy: An assessment and treatment tool for children and their parents in therapy. *Annuals of the American Psychotherapy Association.*

Linares Scott, T.J. (2006). Relapse Prevention Techniques in the Treatment of Childhood Anxiety Disorders: A Case Example. *Journal of Contemporary Psychotherapy.*36, 151.

Iverson, C. (2002). Solution-Focused Brief Therapy. *Advances in Psychiatric Treatment.* 8: 149-156.

Miller, W.R. and Rolliands, S. (2002). Motivational Interviewing: Preparing People for Change. 2nd edition, Guilford Press. New York, New York.

Pavuluri, M.N., Graczyk, P.A., Henry, D.B., Carbray, J.A., Heidenreich, J., & Miklowitz, D.J. (2004). Child-and Famiy-Focused Cognitive-Behavioral Therapy for Pediatric Bipolar Disorder: Development and Preliminary Results. *Journal of American Academy of Child and Adolescent Psychiatry, 43,* 528.

Phelan, T.W. (2004). 1-2-3 Magic: Managing Difficult Behavior in Children 2-12. *Parent Magic Inc., Glen Ellyn, IL.*

Reilly, P.M., Shopshire M.S., Durazzo T.C., & Campbell T.A. (2002). Anger Management for Substance Abuse and Mental Health Clients: Participant Workbook. HHS. Pub. No. (SMA) 08-4210. Rockville, MD: Center for Substance Abuse Treatment, Substance Abuse and Mental Health Services Administration.

Wood, J.J. (2006). Family Involvement in Cognitive-Behavioral Therapy for Children's Anxiety Disorders. *Psychiatric Times, 23.*

About the Author

****

Nate and his wife Debi were married in 1977 and since then have lived in northwestern Minnesota where they have raised 3 children. Nate earned his BA in psychology from Minnesota State University Moorhead, an MS in counseling from North Dakota State University, and a PhD in family psychology from Capella University. Also, he is a Minnesota Licensed Psychologist and a Diplomat with the American Psychotherapy Association. Nate was initially employed in 1982 with A Center for Parents and Children, a child abuse prevention and treatment center, and later joined Lakeland Mental Health Center in 1986. He has been providing therapy, primarily to families, since 1982, helping them to make changes to improve the quality of their lives. Nate has also held the position of supervisor for several different mental health programs, including Children's Mental Health services, during most of his years at Lakeland Mental Health Center. Nate and Debi presently live in Fergus Falls, Minnesota where he has also been an adjunct professor of psychology and counseling for the past 15 years at several area colleges. In addition, he enjoys time with his family, their grandchildren, his dog Rusty, and likes to camp, kayak, and snow shoe on and near the Otter Tail River.

****

Family Interactive Rating Scale

Name:_____ **Date:**_____

Earned points_____ **Total points**_____

☺ Positive

10_____

9_____

8_____

7_____

6_____

5_____

4_____

3_____

2_____

1_____

☹ Negative

Couple's Interactive Rating Scale

Name _____ Date _____

N points_____ B points _____Total points_____

	A	B	C	D	E
Positive					
10					
9					
8					
7					
6					
5					
4					
3					
2					
1					
Negative